Thinking Music Method

Book 1
by **Ruben De Anda**

Printed in the United States of America First Printing, 2020

www.RubenDeAnda.com

Dedication

> **Think** before you ask.
>
> **- Maria de Jesus De Anda**

Contents

Welcome Back

CHAPTERS

Welcome back!

Welcome to Book 1 of the Thinking Music Method. Hopefully you have read the Thinking Music Method Primer and passed the quiz at the end. Knowing the information in the Primer is essential before you move forward on your journey to becoming a better musician.

We will expand upon the Major Scale and see how musicians mostly use this scale. We will also put harmony together with rhythm and create the basic structures that many musical pieces are built upon.

This book will cover the musical concepts of mode, triad, and progression.

 These play buttons allow you to listen to the audio examples throughout my digital books. Please visit soundcloud.com username Thinking Music Method. The direct link is: https://soundcloud.com/user-47217242-526012947 or visit www.ThinkingMusicMethod.com

Mode

CHAPTER 1

Mode

Now that we are more familiar with how a major scale is constructed (see primer), we can discuss how the notes of this scale are arranged.

All the different ways that a musician can play the notes of a major scale are limitless, similarly to all the different ways artists can use the colors of the rainbow.

Here is an example of an artist using colors in a random and splotchy manner, and next to it, the same colors in a cohesive pattern. This chapter will discuss some of the most common ways musicians have played with the notes of the major scale.

To help you understand the next musical concept I will use following train analogy.

Imagine you are in the train pictured here. Each train car is a different color. Inside the first train car, you see that the walls are red. As you move from car to car, the color of the walls changes the mood or feeling of the car. In music this mood shift is referred to as **Mode**. Being in one car is described as being in one mode, and being in another car is another mode.

To create a mode in music, a note from the major scale is emphasized in the same way one color was emphasized in the train car by painting all the walls that color.

This shift in emphasis is similar to what we witness with colors. A shift in colors causes some people to have an emotional response. There have been studies that found when people wear a certain color they feel a certain emotion. A person wearing an orange outfit may feel fun and energetic. The same person wearing green may feel hopeful.

A musician uses this emotional characteristic of mode to help convey different feelings.

To emphasize one note over the others in music means to play that note more frequently or louder than the other notes. This is accomplished by having other musical instruments playing that same emphasized note.

Since there are seven notes in the major scale, there are seven modes. These seven modes are named, Ionian, Dorian, Phrygian, Lydian, Mixolydian, Aeolian, and Locrian.

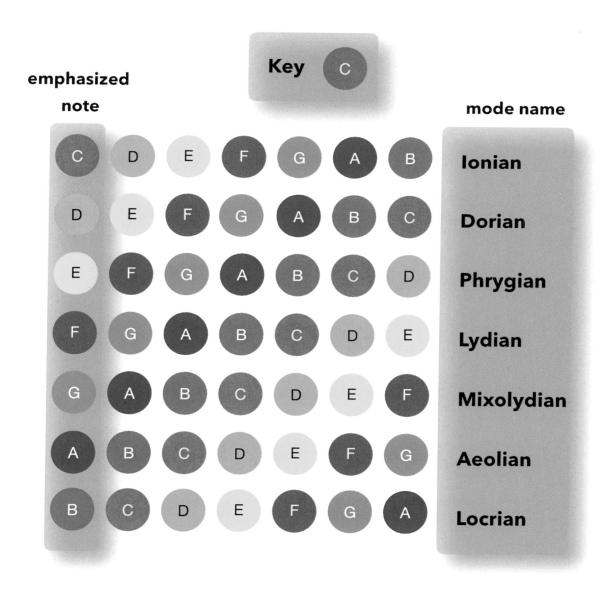

The names of the modes, with the exception of Mixolydian, are associated with locations in Ancient Greece.

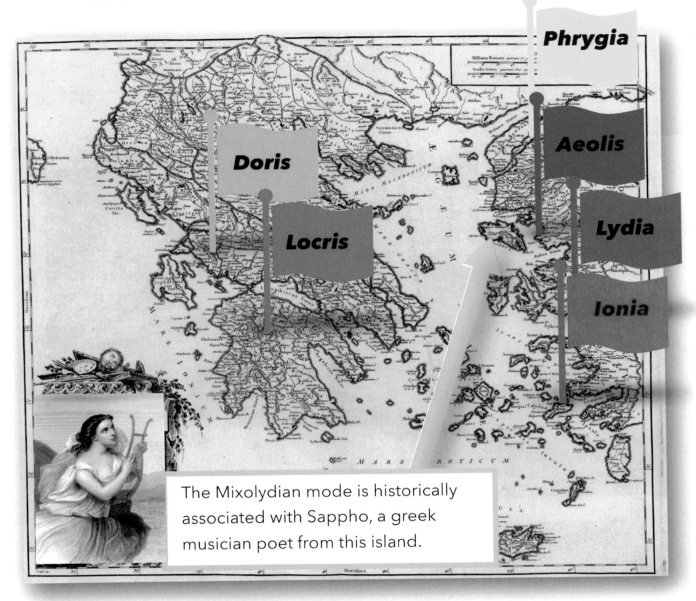

Phrygia

Aeolis

Lydia

Doris

Locris

Ionia

The Mixolydian mode is historically associated with Sappho, a greek musician poet from this island.

The use of modes to create emotional responses varies in different cultures. The following are some common associations I have found between the modes and emotions.

The **Ionian** mode is created by emphasizing the **first** note of the major scale.

Ionian is a popular mode that has a happy and bright feel, commonly found in children's nursery rhymes and holiday carols.

Ionian

1

C D E F G A B

THINKING MUSIC METHOD

dorian

C D E F G A B

√2

Dorian has a cool and sophisticated feel and is incorporated in many Jazz tunes.

D

3

PHRYGIAN

C   D   E   F   G   A   B

E

Phrygian is a dark and peculiar mode that is fashioned in Spanish and metal music.

C D E F G A B

Lyd♯♮an

4

F **Lydian** is used to convey an ethereal mood and is applied in many love songs.

Mixolydian has an energetic sense that is showcased in many rock and dance tunes.

G

C D E F G A B

6

A

The **Aeolian** mode has an introspective and somber feel and is finessed in many sad songs.

LOCRIAN

Locrian has a tense and haunting feel and is manipulated to create suspense and foreboding in horror music.

B

C   D   E   F   G   A   B

Playing Modes

For those students that are able to play notes on a musical instrument, the following exercises will help develop the ear to recognize the different modes.

1. Pick a mode and play the emphasized note.

2. Play other notes from the scale and return to playing the emphasized note.

3. Repeat what you came up with 4 times.

3 min.

examples

In this example Dorian is the mode selected. The D note is played first and last. D with E,F, and A make up the middle.

start D E F D D A F D D

repeat four times

In this example the Mixolydian mode is selected. G is played first and last. G with E,FA, and D are up the middle.

start G D G D E F G A G D G

repeat four times

To make playing with modes more exciting try playing along with the backing tracks I have collected on my Youtube channel. Under my playlists are several videos that explore these modes in different styles. My Youtube channel name is Ruben De Anda.

Mode	3 min	3 min	3 min
Ionian	✓		
Dorian			
Phrygian			
Lydian			
Mixolydian			
Aeolian			
Locrian			

THINKING MUSIC METHOD

Sharpening Your Ears

Here are two listening examples of a traditional French melody. The original melody is in Ionian mode and the second has been transposed to Aeolian mode. Take your time to listen to the two examples several times to hear the differences. This difference is similar to seeing the same picture under a different colored light. Write down whatever sensations, feelings, and memories that come to mind. The process of writing down these descriptions and associating them with the mode will help you identify the mode of a piece of music when listening to it.

Book 1-1

Ionian

Book 1-2

Aeolian

To understand how subtle the differences between the modes are with a more scientific approach, I have inserted this graph which was published in 2011 in the Brazilian Journal of Medical and Biological Research, titled *Manipulating Greek Musical Modes and Tempo Affects Perceived Musical Emotion in Musicians and Non-Musicians*. In the graph D.Ramos, J.L.O. Bueno and E. Bigand explored the emotional effects of musical modes by subjecting people to various musical modes, then asking them how the music made them feel. The participants then made a choice from a list of emotions. The following data was collected.

Table 1. Emotions most frequently chosen by musicians and nonmusicians listening to three pieces in different modes and tempi.

Mode	Tempo (beats per minute)		
	72	108	184
Musicians			
Lydian	Sadness (56.7%)*	Serenity (63.3%)	Happiness (90%)
Ionian	Serenity (63.3%)	Happiness (50%)	Happpiness (96.7%)
Mixolydian	Sadness (53.3%)*	Serenity (66.7%)	Happiness (80%)
Dorian	Sadness (56.7%)	Serenity (60%)	Happiness (73.3%)*
Aeolian	Sadness (53.3%)*	Serenity (46.7%)*	Happiness (53.3%)*
Phrygian	Sadness (70%)	(Serenity 33.3%; Sadness 33.3%; Fear/anger 30%)	(Happines 43.3%; Fear/anger 40%)*
Locrian	Sadness (60%)*	(Serenity 33.3%; Sadness 33.3%)*	Fear/anger (50%)
Nonmusicians			
Lydian	Serenity (63.3%)*	Serenity (56.7%)	Happiness (80%)
Ionian	Serenity (70%)	Happiness (66.7%)	Happpiness (100%)
Mixolydian	Serenity (70%)*	Serenity (50%)	Happiness (83.3%)
Dorian	Sadness (66.7%)	Serenity (50%)	Happiness (43.3%)*
Aeolian	Sadness (83.3%)*	Sadness (60%)*	(Happiness 43.4%; Fear/anger 40%)*
Phrygian	Sadness (63.3%)	(Serenity 33.3%; Sadness 33.3%)	Fear/anger (40%)
Locrian	Fear/anger (56.7%)*	Fear/anger (56.7%)*	Fear/anger (60%)

Data are reported as percent (mean). Pieces that were not associated with a dominant emotion are given in parentheses. *$P \leq 0.005$ compared to musicians' or nonmusicians' responses (ANOVA).

Play the music track titled "Moving Through the Modes". This composition begins in the Ionian mode and will stay in this mode for approximately 16 seconds. After 16 seconds the mode will change to the next mode (Dorian) and so on until the return back to Ionian at 1:52 minutes.

As your ears travel through the modes, take note as to what your brain may associate with each mode to help you distinguish each one.

Keep in mind that as you listen to this track you are hearing seven notes arranged in time where every 15 seconds there is an *emphasis* of a different note.

"Moving Through the Modes"

0:00- 0:16   **Ionian**

0:16- 0:32   **Dorian**

0:32- 0:48   **Phrygian**

0:48- 1:04   **Lydian**

Book 1-3

1:04- 1:20   **Mixolydian**

1:20- 1:36   **Aeolian**

1:36- 1:52   **Locrian**

1:52- 2:08   **Ionian**

It may be a daunting task now to hear what mode is being used in the music you are listening to, but with time these subtle differences will become more and more apparent. At this point, as long as you conceptualize that most music can be organized into seven categories, you will be better equipped to make rational decisions as you make your way to being a musician.

For example, once you learn that Bluegrass music has a majority of its compositions in an Ionian mode, then the Ionian mode is the mode where you will spend most of your time during practice and study.

Triad

CHAPTER 2

Triad

Returning to the analogy of the train, we will discus the concept of triad.

Imagine you are inside the red train car. Inside your suitcase are seven curtains, each one a color of the rainbow. What color curtains do you put up on the window? Your choice of curtain can either **match, compliment, or clash** with the car walls.

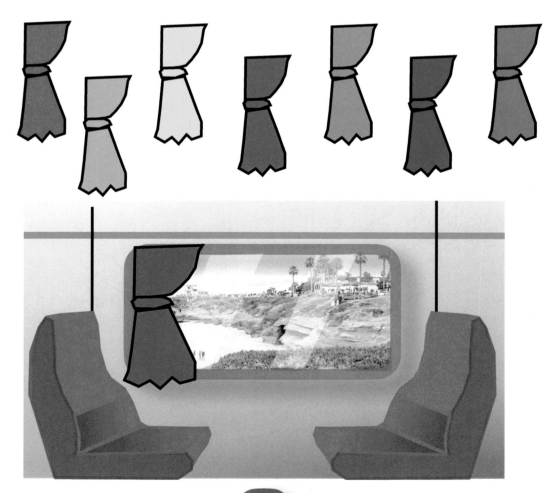

The same principle of matching, complimenting, and clashing occurs between the notes of a major scale. In the Ionian mode in the key of C, the C note **matches** or harmonizes with other C notes. The E and G are two other notes that **complement** the C note. This complementing phenomena in music is called harmonizing. These three notes C,E,G harmonize with each other so well that they are referred to as a **triad**. Notice how the E note is one note away from C, and the G note is one note away from E.

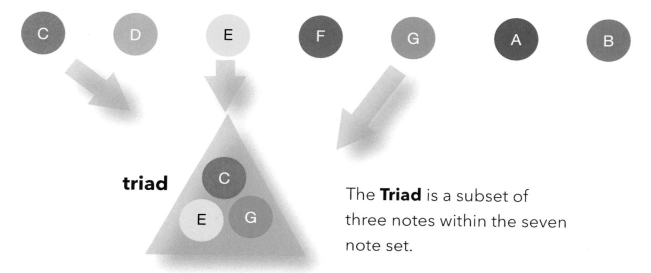

triad

The **Triad** is a subset of three notes within the seven note set.

Each note has its own triad, thus there are seven triads. These triads are built by starting on a note, then grouping it with the note that is one note over from it and then adding another note that is one note away from that note. For example: D, F, and A form a triad.

Each of these seven triads have been given names. They are Tonic, Supertonic, Mediant, Subdominant, Dominant, Submediant, and Leading Tone. The notes within the triad are identified by their numeric relationship to the emphasized note or **Root** note.

Key C

root		3rd		5th			R	3rd	5th	triad name
C	D	E	F	G	A	B	C	E	G	Tonic
D	E	F	G	A	B	C	D	F	A	Supertonic
E	F	G	A	B	C	D	E	G	B	Mediant
F	G	A	B	C	D	E	F	A	C	Subdominant
G	A	B	C	D	E	F	G	B	D	Dominant
A	B	C	D	E	F	G	A	C	E	Submediant
B	C	D	E	F	G	A	B	D	F	Leading tone

Examples of verbiage.

1. The Submediant triad's root note is A.

2. B is the 3rd of the Dominant triad.

3. B,D, and F are the notes that make up the Leading tone triad.

These triangular structures are the fundamental building blocks of almost every musical compositions. Understanding this concept will help you understand the following harmony concepts because they are built upon the triad.

Quality

The next concept used to describe the triad is **quality**. This descriptive concept is similar in the way colors are grouped by the way they are perceived. The colors red, orange, and yellow are usually described as being warm and are grouped together as warm colors. The colors blue, green, and purple are grouped together as cool colors. This grouping of colors can be described as the color's temperature quality. These are imagined descriptions. Colors don't have a temperature, but how colors make people feel seems to be a commonly shared perception.

Likewise, in music, triads can be grouped together by similar qualities. By listening to the the way the triads sound one can

distinguish some similarities. The seven triads are grouped into three qualities.

The Tonic triad has a similar feel as that of the Subdominant triad and the Dominant triad. These three triads are described as having a **Major Quality**.

The Supertonic, Submediant, and Mediant triads all have their own similar feel. These three triads are described as having a **Minor Quality.**

The Leading Tone Triad has its own different feel than all the other six triads and is described as having a **Diminished Quality**.

Some musicians describe the Quality of Major as being bright and happy and Minor as being sad. The Diminished quality has a disturbing feeling about it.

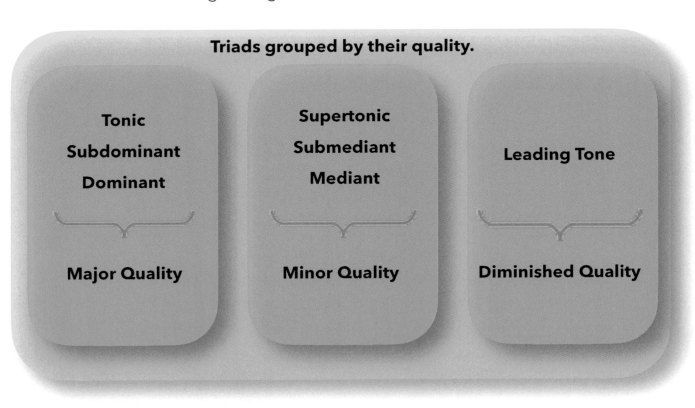

Triads grouped by their quality.

Tonic **Subdominant** **Dominant**	**Supertonic** **Submediant** **Mediant**	**Leading Tone**
Major Quality	**Minor Quality**	**Diminished Quality**

Roman Numerals

ROMAN NUMERALS

1 =	I	5 =	VI
2 =	II	6 =	VI
3 =	III	7 =	VII
4 =	IIII		

To simplify which triad is being used in written form, a number has been assigned to each of the triads. One is assigned to the Tonic triad and so forth to the number seven, to represent the last Leading tone triad.

A system of Roman numerals are used instead of Arabic numbers because Arabic numbers represent other musical information such as indicating which finger to use when playing an instrument.

The quality of the triad is represented by upper case and lower case Roman numerals. Upper case Roman numerals are used for major triads. Lower case Roman numerals are used for minor triads. A small circle following a lower case Roman numeral represents the diminished quality.

R	3rd	5th	triad name	Roman numeral
C	E	G	Tonic	I
D	F	A	Supertonic	ii
E	G	B	Mediant	iii
F	A	C	Subdominant	IV
G	B	D	Dominant	V
A	C	E	Submediant	vi
B	D	F	Leading tone	vii°

Major Quality

Tonic = I

Subdominant = IV

Dominant = V

uppercase Roman numerals

Minor Quality

Supertonic = ii

Mediant = iii

Submediant = vi

lowercase Roman numerals

Diminished Quality

Leading Tone = vii°

lowercase Roman numerals followed by a °

Triad Names

Calling out such triad names as Tonic, Dominant, and or Submediant can become cumbersome especially if you are in the middle of playing music with others. To simplify, musicians will simply refer to each triad by its root note and its quality. For example, the Tonic triad is referred to as "C major" because the root of the Tonic triad is a C and its quality is major. The other triads are referred to as D minor, E minor, F major, G major, A minor, and B diminished.

Tonic triad = C Major

To be more concise, sometimes musicians will only say the root note if the triad is major.

C Major = C

Note of Caution

Please be aware that this last abbreviation can cause confusion to student musicians because "C" can now mean the single note C as well as the triad of notes C,E, and G.

R	3rd	5th	triad name	common name	written abbreviation
C	E	G	**Tonic**	**C major**	**C**
D	F	A	**Supertonic**	**D minor**	**Dm**
E	G	B	**Mediant**	**E minor**	**Em**
F	A	C	**Subdominant**	**F major**	**F**
G	B	D	**Dominant**	**G major**	**G**
A	C	E	**Submediant**	**A minor**	**Am**
B	D	F	**Leading tone**	**B diminished**	**Bdim**

When you do start playing triads on your instrument, pay attention to the quality and learn the differences. A good musician can distinguish between the qualities easily.

Listen to some of the following listening examples and see if you can hear the difference in the quality. It may take a while to hear these differences. Be patient. Your brain will eventually comprehend and identify triad qualities.

Book 1-4

C Major

Book 1-5

F Major

Book 1-6

G Major

Book 1-7

D minor

Book 1-8

E minor

Book 1-9

A minor

Book 1-10

B diminished

Chord

The notes of a triad can be played one of two ways. When triad notes are all played together it is called a **chord**. When the triad notes are played one after another it is called an **arpeggio**.

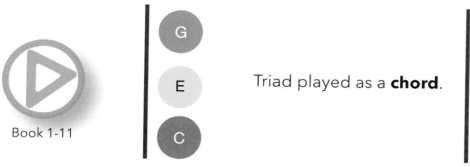

Book 1-11

Triad played as a **chord**.

Book 1-12

Triad played as an **arpeggio**.

Note of Caution

At some point someone started identifying triads as chords. When someone asks, "What chords are used in a piece of music?", they are wondering what triads are being used.

Triads = chords

Jam Time

Before the internet, before TV, before radio, and before record players, one of the pastimes people enjoyed was playing music in a group.

A jam session is an activity where musicians get together to play music with the intent of having **fun**. Improvisation is a large part of a jam session.

The following Jam Tracks are designed for you to practice playing along with musicians who are playing with the corresponding triads. Please refer to the Thinking Music Method Instrument book to help you play along.

As you listen to the tracks of musical accompaniment, play the notes of that triad one at a time. Listen to the Quality of the triad. Listen to how playing the root sounds as compared to playing the 3rd or the 5th notes.

More of these jam tracks will be included in later lessons to give you more experience playing along with different combinations of chords and styles of music.

I
Tonic
C major
C,E,G

Book 1-13

ii
Supertonic
D minor
D,F,A

Book 1-14

iii
Mediant
E minor
E,G, B

Book 1-15

IV
Subdominant
F major
F,A,C

Book 1-16

V
Dominant
G major
G,B,D

Book 1-17

vii
Submediant
A minor
A,C,E

Book 1-18

vii
Leading tone
B dim
B,D,F

Book 1-19

Musicians don't normally jam on the diminished triad, but if this is what turns your ears on, then have fun.

The practice of playing along with tracks also helps you develop the skill of listening and playing right along in tempo with other musicians.

Progression

CHAPTER 3

Progression

Now that we have established the concept of **triad** and **measure,** we can put these two concepts together to create progressions. A **Chord Progression** is a triad or a series of triads repeated within a group of measures.

"Frére Jacques" is a traditional French song. Its Chord Progression has one Triad, in this case being a Tonic triad, and it is played for the duration of 8 measures. Each measure has 4 beats. "Frére Jacques" is an example of a simple chord progression. The audio example includes the measure number to help you hear the duration of eight measures.

Book 1-20

I   "Frére Jacques"

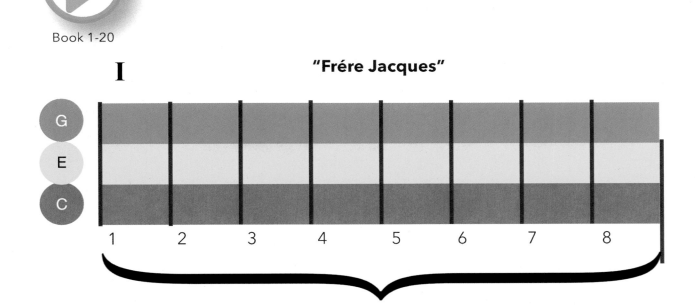

8 measures

A typical blues tune has a more complex chord progression than "Frére Jacques". It uses three triads repeated over 12 measures. These 12 measures are then repeated for the common duration of approximately 3 minutes. It begins with four measures of a tonic triad, two measures of subdominant, two measures of tonic, one measure of dominant, one measure of subdominant, one measure of tonic, then one measure of a dominant. The audio example includes the measure number to help you hear the duration of twelve measures

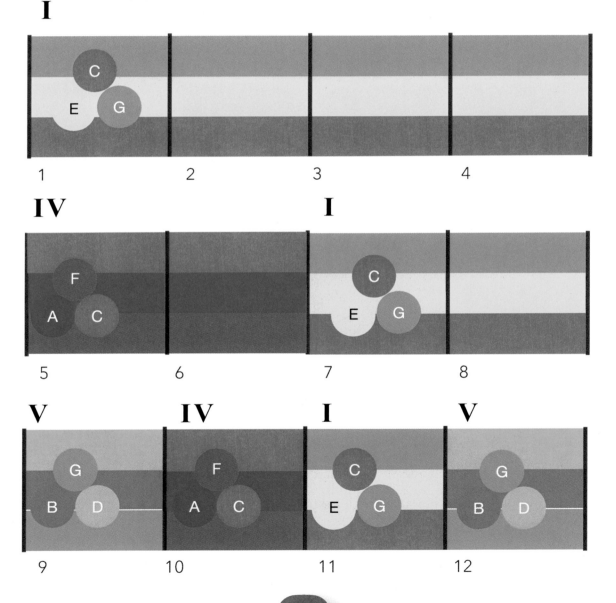

Regarding the previous example of a 12 measure blues progression, the duration of approximately 3 minutes is due to the limitation of space on a vinyl record. The invention of the 45 vinyl record in 1949 could hold a musical composition of only 3 minutes. Therefore, musicians who wanted to make money by selling their music on vinyl had to comply to the 3 minute song length. This length dominated for many decades following this restriction.

It is possible to play this 12 measure progression for as long as you and your musician friends desire. A documentary on Netflix reports that the ensemble ZZ Top played this progression for 3 hours straight, which in my opinion would have been a great way to spend 3 hours with friends.

Playing through a progression is similar to moving through the different colored cars in a train. You will recall that in each train, car the color that is emphasized dictates whether the other colors which are placed in the train match, complement or contrast. Similarly, in a measure, the chord of that measure will dictate whether the note or notes you are playing will harmonize or not.

These decisions about what note to play is what takes up most of a musician's brain power, whether the player is conscious about it or not. With repeated practice, this decision process will become subconscious, much like most of us speak without thinking of the grammar of our sentences.

All musical pieces have a chord progression, from a simple one-chord progression to a mind-bogglingly complex progression. Being able to identify the difference will help you choose which pieces of music to study first. Generally, you will want to study the simpler progressions then gradually move to more complex chord progressions. With this information you will be able to make better decisions on how to train your brain, ears and hands.

As we continue through these lessons, please be mindful of the chord progression.

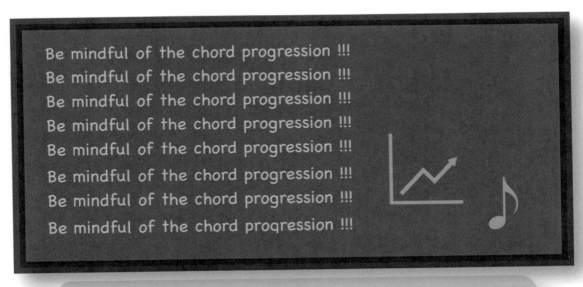

Be mindful of the chord progression !!!
Be mindful of the chord progression !!!
Be mindful of the chord progression !!!
Be mindful of the chord progression !!!
Be mindful of the chord progression !!!
Be mindful of the chord progression !!!
Be mindful of the chord progression !!!
Be mindful of the chord progression !!!

Repeat 100 times either by writing or saying:
"Be mindful of the progression."

Rhythm

CHAPTER 4

Division

In the Thinking Music Method Primer we learned how beats are grouped into measures. The next aspect of rhythm is knowing that a beat can be divided into smaller units of time like a foot can be divided into inches.

BEAT

 To divide a beat means that a musician plays more than one note in the time of one beat.

 Dividing a beat into two equal parts allows for two notes to be played, one after the other in one beat.

 Dividing a beat into three equal parts allows for three notes to be played in one beat.

 Dividing a beat into four equal parts allows for four notes to be played one after another in one beat.

Book 1-24

Beat divided into four parts.

One po-ta-to   two po-ta-to   three po-ta-to   four po-ta-to

The syllables of the word "potato" are used to represent the second, third, and fourth parts of the beat.

Some music schools use e-and-a to count the divisions. However using these vowels repetitively can become a "blurry" mess making it difficult to hear the divisions clearly. It is easier to distinguish the divisions with the percussiveness of the syllables of po-ta-to.

Counting

The beat can be divided in any number of ways, but the most common are 2, 3, and 4 notes per beat. Book II goes further on explaining how these divisions are notated and practiced. Listen to how each beat division is counted and how the even distribution of each syllable is pronounced.

Beat divided into two parts.

Book 1-22

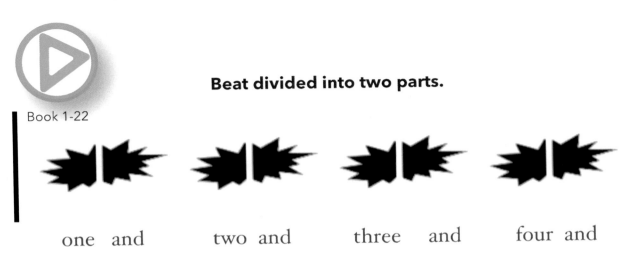

one   and   two and   three   and   four and

The word "and" is used to represent the second part of the beat.

Beat divided into three parts.

Book 1-23

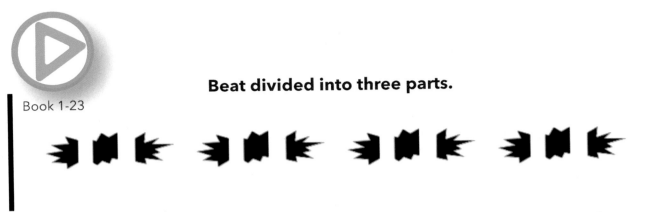

one tri-plet   two tri-plet   three tri-plet   four tri-plet

The two syllables of the word triplet "trip-let" is used to represent the second part and third part of the beat.

Phrase

We are now going to zoom out and look at a larger rhythmic unit called a phrase. A **phrase** is a musical sentence that usually lasts a few measures. It is most common for phrases to be about four measures long.

four-measure phrase

In the example of "Frére Jacques" p.38, I would describe the melody as having two four-measure phrases. In the typical blues tune on p. 39, I would describe the structure as having three four-measure phrases.

Most music seems to have an obsession with durations of four, much like we obsess with making many objects with four sides. Recognizing this commonality will help you learn music more efficiently.

When you approach a piece of music, count the measures and pay attention to how many four-measure phrases are being used. This grouping of measure is a good way of establishing *landmarks* to help you know *when* you are in the music.

In the jazz standard *Fly Me to the Moon*, I would describe this progression as having a 32 measures structure, divided into two similar 16-measure sections. Each section composed of four four-measure phrases. This is an example of a more complicated chord progression.

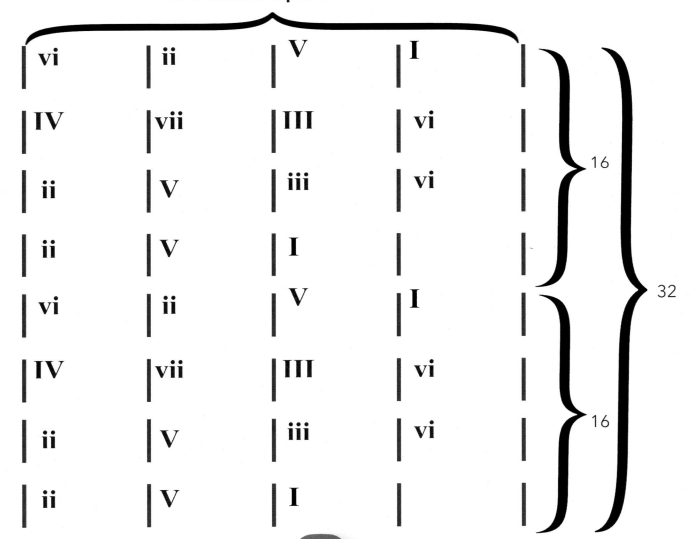

Counting out Loud

Most of us organize time by years, months, weeks, days, hours, minutes and seconds. In music-time, time is organized by beats, measure and phrases.

The following exercises will help the mind recognize music-time by verbally counting out the rhythm to the beat.

3 min.

Pick a comfortable tempo with a metronome and read the rhythms out loud. Be sure to say the beat number (1,2,3,4) right with the beat of your metronome. Repeat for three minutes. When you feel confident, increase the tempo and record your progress.

1.

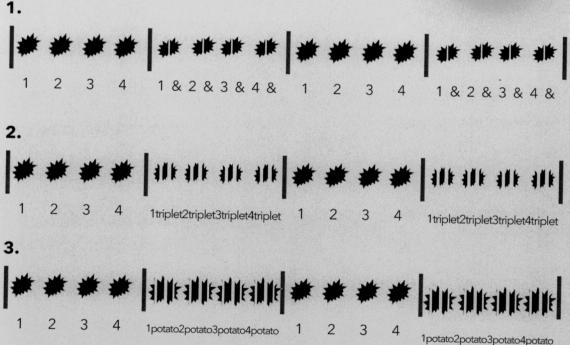

1   2   3   4   1 & 2 & 3 & 4 &   1   2   3   4   1 & 2 & 3 & 4 &

2.

1   2   3   4   1triplet2triplet3triplet4triplet   1   2   3   4   1triplet2triplet3triplet4triplet

3.

1   2   3   4   1potato2potato3potato4potato   1   2   3   4   1potato2potato3potato4potato

4.

1 2 3 4 1triplet2triplet3triplet4triplet 1potato2potato3potato4potato 1 & 2 & 3 & 4 &

5.

1 2 3 4 1 & 2 & 3potato4potato 1 & 2 & 3potato4potato 1 & 2 & 3 & 4 &

6.

1 2 3 4 1triplet2triplet 3 4 1 2 3triplet4triplet 1 2 3 4

exercise	2 min at 80bpm	2 min at 100bpm	2 min at 120bpm
1			
2			
3			
4			
5			
6			

Review

CHAPTER 5

Quiz

1. How many modes are there in music? _____

2. Each note in a major scale harmonizes with two other notes forming a _____.

3. Triads are grouped into three _____.

4. The G major triad is usually abbreviated as _____.

5. The D minor triad is usually abbreviated as _____.

6. The Roman numeral abbreviation for the submediant triad is _____.

7. A _____ is a series of triads repeated within a group of measures.

8. Emphasis of one note over the rest of the notes in a scale creates a sensation known as _____.

9. The most common divisions of a beat are 2, 3, and ____.

10. It is common for melodies to have a _____ measure phrase.

Summary

I hope the concepts covered so far are helping you visualize the structures present in the sounds we call music. We started with a single key-note upon which a scale of seven notes was derived. This set of seven notes is the major scale. Emphasizing one of these seven notes creates a mode. The modes were used to evoke different feelings. Each note of the scale harmonizes with two other specific notes from that same scale creating a triad.

Beat is the pulse felt in music. Repeating groups of accented and unaccented beats create a meter. One of these groups is referred to as a measure. Triads are played in patterns in groups of measures to create chord progressions.

harmony   **music**   **rhythm**

progression

triad

phrase

measure

mode

meter

scale

tempo

key

beat

Reference

	root		3rd		5th			R	3rd	5th	triad name	Roman numeral

Key C

root		3rd		5th			R	3rd	5th	triad name	Roman numeral
C	D	E	F	G	A	B	C	E	G	Tonic	I
D	E	F	G	A	B	C	D	F	A	Supertonic	ii
E	F	G	A	B	C	D	E	G	B	Mediant	iii
F	G	A	B	C	D	E	F	A	C	Subdominant	IV
G	A	B	C	D	E	F	G	B	D	Dominant	V
A	B	C	D	E	F	G	A	C	E	Submediant	vi
B	C	D	E	F	G	A	B	D	F	Leading tone	vii°

Major Quality

Tonic = I

Subdominant = IV

Dominant = V

Minor Quality

Supertonic = ii

Mediant = iii

Submediant = vi

Diminished Quality

Leading Tone = vii°

Print and cut out these flashcards and study them daily.

Mode	Ionian
Dorian	Phrygian
Lydian	Mixolydian

THINKING MUSIC METHOD

Ionian is the mode created when emphasizing the first note of a major scale.

Mode is the emphasis of one note from the major scale.

Phrygian is the mode created when emphasizing the third note of a major scale.

Dorian is the mode created when emphasizing the second note of a major scale.

Mixolydian is the mode created when emphasizing the fifth note of a major scale.

Lydian is the mode created when emphasizing the fourth note of a major scale.

THINKING MUSIC METHOD

Aeolian	Locrian
Triad	Tonic
Super Tonic	Mediant

Locrian is the mode created when emphasizing the sixth note of a major scale.

Aeolian is the mode created when emphasizing the sixth note of a major scale.

The **Tonic** is a triad based upon the first note of the major scale.

A **Triad** is group of three harmonious notes.

The **Mediant** is a triad based upon the third note of the major scale.

The **Super Tonic** is a triad based upon the second note of the major scale.

Subdominant	Dominant
Submediant	Leading Tone
Quality	Progression

The **Dominant** is a triad based upon the fifth note of the major scale.

The **Subdominant** is a triad based upon the fourth note of the major scale.

The **Leading Tone** is a triad based upon the seventh note of the major scale.

The **Submdiant** is a triad based upon the sixth note of the major scale.

Progression is the order of the triads in a musical composition.

Quality is the particular sound of a triad. Can be either major, minor or diminished.

The Primer introduces you to basic musical concepts. Choose the instrument book that corresponds to your instrument of choice. Continue your journey thorough books 1,2, and 3. More musical examples that will prepare you for the world of music are in my Tune Books.

Index

	primer	book 1	book 2
arpeggio		33	
beat	30	44	28
chord		33	11
harmony	20	23	45
key	20	5	45
major scale	22	2	45
measure	36	38	28
meter	37		57
mode		2	56
phrase		47	12
progression		38	10
quality		27	17
rhythm	30	44	28
scale	21	2	46
tempo	32		31
triad		23	11

THINKING MUSIC METHOD

Thank you!

Thank you to all my music teachers and to all my music students.

Thank you to all who helped contribute to this book especially:

Leticia S. De Anda - photographer

Norma De Anda Nguyen

Sandra De Anda

William Ostrie

Bonny Tinling

Linda Bannan

Mike Bannan

Nina Hofstadler

Francisco Antonorsi

Christy Johnson, editor catalystchristy@gmail.com

Support

Ruben lives with his wife and cat in Southern California. He has brought a love and deeper understanding of music to numerous students. Donations to support this work and expanding series can be directed to…

https://www.patreon.com/RubenDeAnda

or

my PayPal account: deandaguitar@gmail.com

Thank you!

THINKING MUSIC METHOD

Made in the USA
Las Vegas, NV
31 July 2023

75491904R00045